Beltane

a fun book for Pagan children

MW01277307

Canto Silva

Text and concept, (C) Siena E. Stone, 2024
Images, Public Domain

More fun books in the
Fun Books for Pagan Children Series:

Imbolc
Beltane
Lammas

And soon:
Mabon
Yule
Ostara
Litha

In this book, you will find:

Beltane in the Wheel of the Year

Beltane is one of the eight holidays of the Wheel of the Year.

These holidays are called Sun Days because they happen as the Earth tuns around the sun.

We imagine Sun Days as pegs on a wheel that turns with the Earth through the year.

Label this
Wheel of the Year

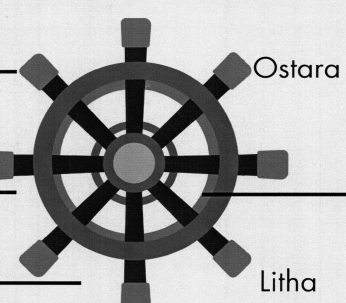

_____

_____

Ostara

_____

_____

Litha

_____

Lammas

We celebrate Beltane on May the 1st, smack in between Ostara and Litha.

Beltane is in the very middle of spring.

On May the 1st, people also celebrate a holiday called May Day. It's a celebration of workers, kind of like Labor Day.

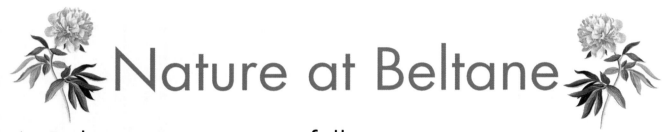

Nature at Beltane

At Beltane, nature is in full spring.

The grass is green, fruit trees are blooming and there are flowers everywhere.

The days get longer and the nights get shorter.

It also starts getting warm. You may start wearing lighter clothes.

Animals are very busy. Many have young families that need food and care.

You find bugs everywhere, crawling and flying. The air is full of buzz and song.

In many places, the last frosts come in May.

The hawthorn is a tree that blooms in May.

There is a legend that says that there is no more frost after it blooms.

Some people call it May Blossom, like in the image on the right.

MAY BLOSSOM

Beltane is on May the 1st.
Write here other dates in
May that are important to
you:

_____

- -

_____

_____

- -

_____

_____

- -

_____

_____

- -

_____

_____

- -

_____

May crossword puzzle

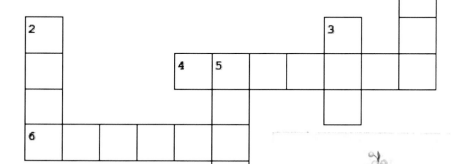

Down

1. Many of these bloom in May
2. Insects and other small critters
3. It gets longer in May
5. It gets shorter in May

Across

4. Many of these have families in May
6. Beltane is in the middle of this season

Beltane cards

Cut them out, write on the back and give them to your friends to wish them a happy Beltane.

The Maypole Dance.

Pan

Pan with his pipes
Made trees to grow.
Flowers to bud.
And rivers to flow.

Famous Fairies

"Away to the woodlands, away—
To dance to the honor of May."

Deities of Beltane

Beltane is special because it celebrates the union between a god and a goddess.

Beltane gods are young men. Many are gods of the wilderness. Some have horns.

Beltane goddesses are young women. Many are goddesses of flowers. They often wear flower crowns.

The Lord and the Lady

Some people see the Lord as a god that represents all male gods. They see the Lady as a goddess who represents all goddesses.

Other people see Him as the Sun. They see the Lady as the Moon.

The Lord and the Lady love each other. When they are together, magick happens. They are stronger, happier and more powerful. They make a good team!

Fig. 39.

The Lord and the Lady get married at Beltane and nature celebrates with flowers. They have a handfasting ceremony. That's a Pagan wedding.

During the ceremony, they jump the broom. Look at the picture below. The bride is jumping the broom while holding her groom's hand.

CUT III.   Marrying over the Broomstick.

Symbols of the Lord:
- Animals with horns, like deer and goats
- The Sun
- Oak trees, oak leaves and acorns
- The color white
- Wands and knifes

Symbols of the Lady:
- Roses
- The Moon
- The Earth
- A star
- Cauldrons and goblets
- The color red

Symbols of Their wedding:
- Flower garlands
- A broom
- Braids
- The colors red and white together
- A wand and a goblet together

Illustrations - Caldecott
#18, CHP (1885)
The Great Panjandrum Himself

Lord and Lady Word Search

S	G	H	R	G	B	E	M	E	E	H	R	B	T
E	N	O	T	N	N	N	O	A	D	N	E	E	M
P	I	W	T	H	O	E	T	M	E	E	H	L	E
E	P	E	T	A	I	V	I	E	R	E	T	T	O
V	M	N	O	N	T	O	L	A	A	T	E	A	T
O	U	B	L	D	A	A	G	B	T	M	G	N	B
L	J	E	A	F	R	T	N	T	R	R	O	E	E
M	D	I	D	A	B	A	I	O	B	O	T	T	H
O	N	E	Y	S	E	U	D	A	T	J	O	D	O
E	I	O	N	T	L	L	D	I	N	L	S	M	N
W	G	O	N	I	E	N	E	N	R	A	G	N	N
B	L	A	I	N	C	G	W	U	D	E	N	I	E
I	N	D	U	G	M	D	R	O	L	E	M	D	F
N	A	P	U	N	I	O	N	T	G	Y	Y	U	N

LOVE
LORD
WEDDING
UNION
HANDFASTING
TEAM
LADY
BROOM
TOGETHER
JUMPING
CELEBRATION
BELTANE

Play this puzzle online at : https://thewordsearch.com/puzzle/7603755/

Make a Lord and Lady lucky bracelet

These bracelets are made in spring for luck. You wear it until it is so old that it breaks.
The red and white yarns twisted together represent the union of the Lord and the Lady at Beltane.

You will need two pieces of yarn, one white and one red. They must be long enough to go four times around your wrist.

- Put both pieces of yarn together and ask someone to hold them by one end.
- Twist the two pieces of yarn around each other.
- When you are done, bring the ends together. The yarn will curl on itself.
- Make a knot on the open end. Put around your wrist and make a knot to close.

Flora

Flora is a Roman goddess. She is the goddess of flowers, youth and spring.

Flora is a young woman. She makes sure there are flowers in spring.

When She walks, flowers sprout around her feet. Trees bloom when She touches them.

She always wears a flower crown.

Flora's name means "flower".

When we talk about the
flora of a place, we mean
all the plants that grow in
that place.

Her symbols are:
- Flowers
- Flower crowns
- The May bush

Make a felt flower crown

A felt flower crown is fun to make and even more fun to wear!

You will need:
- Craft felt of different colors
- One ribbon long enough to go around your head and down your back a bit
- Tacky glue or fabric glue
- The patterns in the next page
- A marker

Instructions:
- Cut out the paper patterns.
- Put one pattern on top of a piece of felt and draw a line around the edge with the marker.
- Repeat this with all the patters in different color felts.
- Cut the felt flowers using the lines you drew as a guide.
- Glue one small flower to one big flower to make 3D flowers.
- Glue the 3D flowers to the ribbon. Start in the center of the ribbon and move towards the sides.
- When you have enough flowers to go around your hear, you are done!
- Tie the ribbon around your head to wear your crown.

Pan

Pan is a Greek god. He protects wild animals and plants, as well as shepherds and their flock.

He is a young man with a human body, goat legs and horns on his head.

He lives in caves in the forest.

Pan's legs were like a goat's, but he played such music that the nymphs would have no one else to play for their dancing

Pan is a happy god, but he is also a fighter. He can shout in a special way that makes everybody afraid. This fear is called panic, after Him.

He loves music and plays many different types of flutes. He made a special one out of reeds. It's called "panpipes".

Pan's symbols are:

- Horns
- Panpipes!
- Ivy
- Reeds
- Goats

23   PAN

Pan Word Search

S	E	R	E	G	S	A	V	T	N	S	I	S	V
V	S	E	A	I	P	A	N	P	I	P	E	S	S
E	S	C	T	H	O	R	N	S	O	Y	C	A	G
I	C	E	I	S	H	A	I	F	V	I	I	O	Y
N	I	E	S	S	N	T	O	I	S	V	N	I	R
R	T	A	E	P	E	R	E	U	S	R	A	A	C
T	A	S	E	R	E	N	M	N	D	W	P	S	C
E	O	R	I	S	G	R	D	A	R	E	N	O	A
E	G	E	T	O	E	R	T	E	E	N	S	N	V
V	I	E	W	E	W	I	L	D	H	E	C	H	E
E	E	S	D	E	E	R	E	N	P	S	E	P	R
E	P	R	N	I	D	T	S	P	E	O	H	R	C
E	C	E	E	O	N	R	O	F	H	S	S	P	S
P	U	N	C	H	A	S	E	P	S	H	E	A	H

PANPIPES
IVY
PANIC
GREECE
REEDS
GOAT
WILD
HORNS
SHEPHERDS
FOREST
MUSIC
CAVE

Play this puzzle online at : https://thewordsearch.com/puzzle/7604223/

Pan coloring page

Bel

Bel is a Celtic god of light, fire and the sun. He is also called Belenus. His name means "shiny".

He likes riding horses and driving horse carriages.

Beltane is named after Him.

Bel brings the warmth of the summer and he starts working at Beltane.

Bel's fire is healing and burns bad things.

Bel's symbols:

- The Sun
- A wheel
- A charriot
- Fire
- The metal Gold
- The colors red, orange and yellow
- A sunburst (that's the sun with rays of light coming out of it, like in the image on this page.)

Bel Coloring Page

Cossword Puzzle

Across

4. Cars have four of these.

5. The star that our planet turns around.

6. This element burns things, and gives light and heat.

7. An expensive yellow metal that people use to make jewelry.

Down

1. Bel likes riding these.

2. An electric discharge in a storm.

3. A holiday named after Bel.

5. Bel means this.

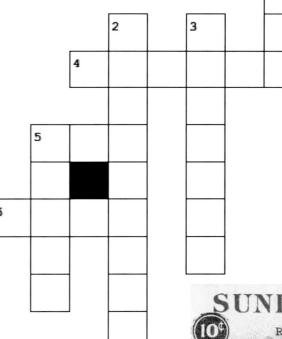

SUNFLOWE

10¢ RED

The Fae

The Fae are small people-like magickal beings. They are also called Fairies, Fair Folk and Good Neighbors. They love Beltane.

Just like people and animals, some Fae are nice and some are naughty. They also have good days and bad days. They can be helpful or be up to mischief.

People think they have wings, but many don't.

The Fae don't like people who are nasty or rude to them.

They like people who are polite and give them offerings (gifts). Offerings for the Fae can be:

- Juice
- Cake or bread
- Honey
- Milk or cream
- Beads or shiny things
- Flowers
- Pretty rocks

You just leave your offering in a small bowl on the windowsill or outside the front door.

Celebrating Beltane

- Take a Beltane walk. How many different flowers can you find? Take pictures of them.
- Wear a flower crown.
- Jump over a broom, a bonfire or a candle.
- Make a Beltane Spoon Cake.
- Make lucky Lord and Lady yarn bracelets for your friends.
- Eat your first cherry or strawberry of the year. Make a wish!
- Dance around the May Pole!
- Plant something in your garden.
- Leave an offering for the Fae.

Beltane Spoon Cake

A spoon cake is a very soft cake that breaks if you cut it, so you have to eat it with a spoon.

The Beltane Spoon Cake is made with strawberries. Strawberries are a May food and they are delicious! You can use frozen or fresh strawberries. Smash them with a fork. It's fun!

Ingredients:

- ½ cup butter (1 stick), melted
- 1 cup strawberries
- ⅔ cup brown sugar
- ½ cup whole milk
- ½ teaspoon kosher salt
- 1 cup all-purpose flour
- 1 teaspoon baking powder

Beltane Spoon Cake

Instructions:

- Heat oven to 350 degrees. Grease a baking dish with butter.
- On a plate, mash the berries and mix with half the brown sugar.
- Separately, mix the melted butter, remaining ⅓ cup brown sugar, milk and salt.
- Add the flour and baking powder. Continue until the batter is smooth. Put the batter in the greased baking dish.
- Put the strawberries and their juice on top of the cake batter. Bake 20-25 minutes. It's ready when a toothpick comes out clean in the center.
- Serve warm with ice cream.

Strawberry

What Beltane teaches us

Beltane is a celebration of life. Plants and animals are working to create the future bounty of summer. Beltane teaches us that when we live fully, we make a beautiful, happy, abundant world.

Beltane also shows us that when many come together, they can do much more than alone. The Lord and the Lady are stronger together and the ribbons in the May Pole make a beautiful pattern that one ribbon cannot make alone.

Have you ever joined a team to do something you couldn't do alone? Write about it in the following pages.

Muguet
Porte Bonheur

more
Fun Books for Pagan Children
by Canto Silva

Lammas
a fun book for Pagan children

Canto Silva

Samhain
a fun book for Pagan children

Canto Silva

Imbolc
a fun book for Pagan children

Canto Silva

available at Amazon

16381810R00031

Manufactured by Amazon.ca
Acheson, AB